NORTH CAROLINA
TAR HEELS

BY ALEX MONNIG

Published by ABDO Publishing Company, PO Box 298166, Minneapolis, MN 55439. Copyright © 2012 by Abdo Consulting Group, Inc. International copyrights reserved in all countries. No part of this book may be reproduced in any form without written permission from the publisher. SportsZone™ is a trademark and logo of ABDO Publishing Company.

Printed in the United States of America,
North Mankato, Minnesota
102011
012012

Editor: Chrös McDougall
Copy Editor: Anna Comstock
Design and production: Craig Hinton

Photo Credits: Focus on Sport/Getty Images, cover; Kathy Willens/AP Images, 1; Manny Millan/Sports Illustrated/Getty Images, 4, 42 (bottom left); Heinz Kluetmeier/Sports Illustrated/Getty Images, 6; Rich Clarkson/Sports Illustrated/Getty Images, 8; AP Images, 11, 22; Collegiate Images/Getty Images, 12, 15, 42 (top left), 43 (top); William P. Straeter/AP Images, 17, 42 (top right); Doug Mills/AP Images, 18; WAS/AP Images, 21; Ed Reinke/AP Images, 25, 42 (bottom right); Bob Jordan/AP Images, 26; Chuck Burton/AP Images, 29; Mary Ann Chastain/AP Images, 31; Grant Halverson/AP Images, 33; Jeff Roberson/AP Images, 34; Eric Gay/AP Images, 37; Gerry Broome/AP Images, 38; Paul Sancya/AP Images, 41, 43 (bottom); Sporting News Archive/Getty Images, 44

Design elements: Matthew Brown/iStockphoto

Library of Congress Cataloging-in-Publication Data
Monnig, Alex.
  North Carolina Tar Heels / by Alex Monnig.
     p. cm. -- (Inside college basketball)
  Includes index.
  ISBN 978-1-61783-286-4
  1. University of North Carolina at Chapel Hill--Basketball--History--Juvenile literature. 2. North Carolina Tar Heels (Basketball team)--History--Juvenile literature. I. Title.
  GV885.43.U54M66 2012
  796.323'6309756565--dc23
  [B]
                    2011038469

TABLE OF CONTENTS

DEC 2012

The Tar Heels' Michael Jordan takes the game-winning shot against Georgetown during the 1982 NCAA Tournament finals.

JORDAN'S JUMPER

THE UNIVERSITY OF NORTH CAROLINA MEN'S BASKETBALL PROGRAM WAS FOUNDED IN 1911. SINCE THEN, IT HAD BUILT ITSELF INTO ONE OF THE TOP COLLEGE BASKETBALL PROGRAMS IN THE NATION. THE TAR HEELS HAD EVEN WON THE NATIONAL COLLEGIATE ATHLETIC ASSOCIATION (NCAA) TOURNAMENT CHAMPIONSHIP IN 1957.

Dean Smith took over as the Tar Heels' coach in 1961–62. With talented players such as forwards Billy Cunningham, Larry Miller, and Charles Scott, and guards Phil Ford and Bob Lewis, Smith and North Carolina racked up the wins. But through the 1980–81 season, they always fell short in the end.

Smith guided his teams to the Final Four six times. But they lost three times in the national semifinals and three times in the final. One of those near-championship misses came in 1981. The Tar Heels reached the finals of the NCAA Tournament, but there they lost to the Indiana Hoosiers.

North Carolina's Michael Jordan goes for a layup while Georgetown center Patrick Ewing defends in the 1982 NCAA Tournament finals.

The 1981–82 team was different. It had blazed through the regular season and the Atlantic Coast Conference (ACC) tournament with a 27–2 record. Junior forward James Worthy led the Tar Heels with 15.6 points per game. Sophomore forward Sam Perkins averaged 14.3 points and 7.8 rebounds per game. North Carolina also featured an exciting, athletic freshman guard named Michael Jordan. He averaged 13.5 points per game.

North Carolina was no stranger to close games that season. In fact, three of the team's first four NCAA Tournament games were decided by five points or fewer. But all of those close games ended with North Carolina wins. That set up a championship game against the Georgetown Hoyas and their star freshman center, Patrick Ewing. And like so many of North Carolina's previous games, it all came down to the final moments.

The game went back and forth. Georgetown had a narrow 32–31 lead at halftime. Neither team was able to build much momentum in the second half. Worthy was pouring in the points for the Tar Heels. But Ewing was scoring, rebounding, and blocking shots for the Hoyas. Fortunately for the Tar Heels, Ewing was blocking a few too many shots. North Carolina's first eight points came from four goaltending calls on Ewing. The Tar Heels did not make a basket of their own until more than eight minutes had passed in the game.

BIG LOUD CROWD

The 1982 NCAA championship game had the highest attendance of any college basketball game ever at the time. North Carolina and Georgetown battled in the Superdome in New Orleans, Louisiana. That stadium is the home of the National Football League's New Orleans Saints. The attendance of 61,612 almost doubled the total of the previous high. The game started a trend of hosting the NCAA Tournament's Final Four and national championship games in large sporting arenas and stadiums.

JORDAN'S JUMPER

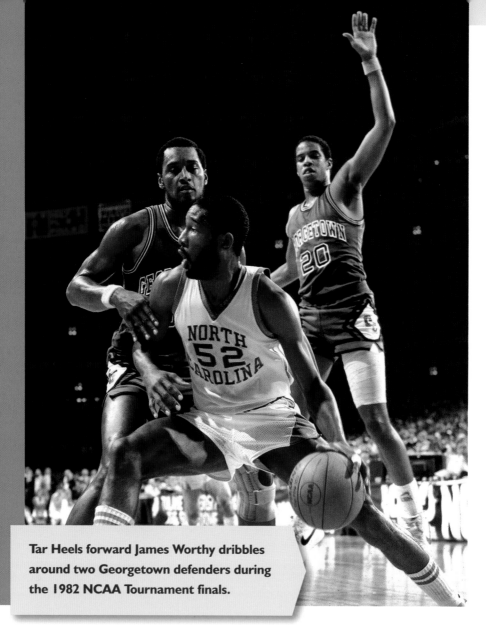

Tar Heels forward James Worthy dribbles around two Georgetown defenders during the 1982 NCAA Tournament finals.

Late in the second half, North Carolina led 61–58. But the Hoyas scored on two straight possessions to take a 62–61 lead with 57 seconds left. It was looking like the Tar Heels would come up one win short of the title for the second straight year. But then, with just 15 seconds left, North Carolina senior point guard Jimmy Black found Jordan open to the left of the basket.

The Hoyas' defense had left the freshman open from the difficult shooting angle. They were more worried about making sure Worthy and Perkins were well guarded. Jordan received the pass. He then rose and released a jump shot that swished through the hoop to give the Tar Heels a one-point lead.

Some thought Georgetown would call a timeout to draw up one final play. Instead, the Hoyas inbounded the ball and headed up the court. Georgetown point guard Fred Brown dribbled to the top of the key. He pump-faked before trying to pass the ball to guard Sleepy Floyd. Brown passed the ball to his right. But Floyd had cut toward the basket. The only person standing there to receive the pass was Worthy. The North Carolina forward raced down the left sideline dribbling the ball.

The Hoyas were able to foul Worthy to stop the clock. He missed both free throws. That gave Georgetown one more chance. But Floyd's long-range shot with

GAME OF GREATS

North Carolina coach Dean Smith said he knew several Tar Heels had bright futures in basketball when he spoke about the talent on the court after the 1982 NCAA championship game. His team featured three future National Basketball Association (NBA) players on its roster for the final. Sam Perkins played 17 years in the NBA. James Worthy went on to play 12 seasons with the Los Angeles Lakers. He made seven All-Star teams in a row starting in 1986, and he won three NBA championships.

Michael Jordan went on to superstardom with the Chicago Bulls and the Washington Wizards. He won four Most Valuable Player (MVP) Awards, he was an All-Star 14 times, and he won six NBA titles with the Bulls. Many consider him the best basketball player ever. In 1997, Worthy and Jordan were named as two of the NBA's 50 greatest players of all time.

JORDAN'S JUMPER

two seconds left fell in front of the basket. The game was over. Smith had won his first national title as the Tar Heels' coach.

"I thought it was one of the great basketball games," he said. "There was tremendous talent on the court."

Jordan would go on to become one of the greatest professional basketball players of all time. In that 1982 North Carolina championship, he scored 16 points and grabbed a team-high nine rebounds. But he was still relatively unknown on North Carolina's star-studded team. After the game, everyone wanted to know why the freshman took the team's final shot.

"During the timeout, coach told me I was the one to get the shot," Jordan said. "I tried not to think about it. I wasn't nervous. I felt good from that spot right there. It was in my range. I didn't see it go in. I didn't look at the ball at all. I just prayed."

Worthy made 13 of his 17 shots and finished the game with a career-high 28 points. He was named the Final Four's Most Outstanding Player. Perkins added 10 points to the team's total. And Worthy, Perkins, Jordan, and Black were all named to the All-Tournament team.

DEAN'S DREAM TEAM

"I've thought about [how it would feel to win a championship], but it wasn't that big a thing. . . . It was important for the team to win, not me. It is ridiculous for a coach to set a goal for himself to win a national championship. It is important for the team to have goals." —Dean Smith, after leading North Carolina to the 1982 NCAA championship

It was North Carolina's first title since 1957 and Smith's first in four trips to the championship game. He would continue to guide the Tar Heels to success for another 15 seasons before retiring in 1997. This included winning another NCAA title in 1993.

Smith helped make North Carolina one of the most successful and popular college basketball teams in the country during his 36 years as head coach. But even with his blueprint for success and a host of talented players, things did not always go according to plan for the Tar Heels. The school had to weather some bumpy patches after Smith's retirement before one of its own came back to return the team to glory.

JORDAN'S JUMPER

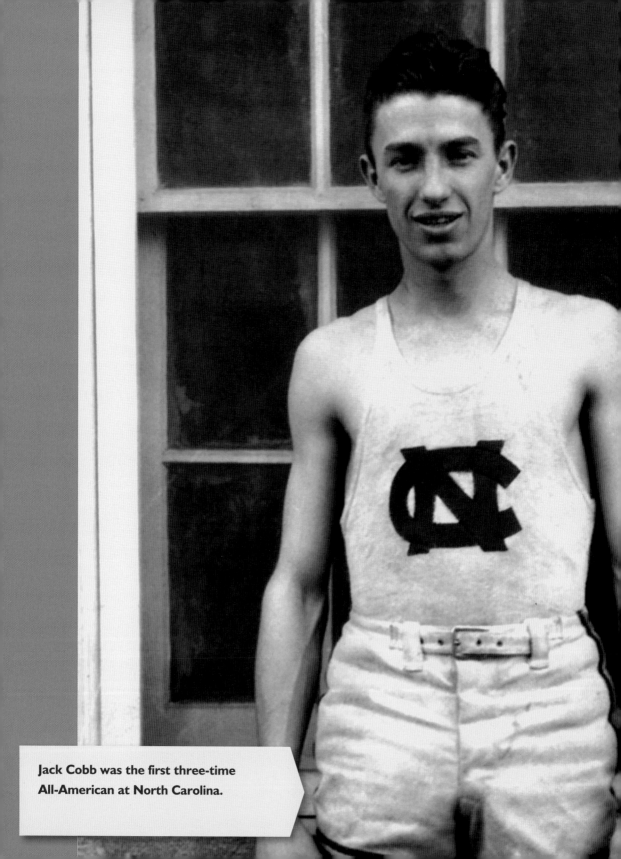

Jack Cobb was the first three-time
All-American at North Carolina.

2

THE EARLY YEARS

THE TAR HEELS STARTED THEIR WINNING WAYS IN THEIR VERY FIRST GAME. ON JANUARY 27, 1911, THEY DEFEATED VIRGINIA CHRISTIAN 42–41 FOR THE FIRST VICTORY IN SCHOOL HISTORY. NORTH CAROLINA FINISHED THE SEASON WITH A 7–4 RECORD.

That first game set the tone for the next several decades. North Carolina finished with more wins than losses in seven of its first 11 seasons. In 1921, the Tar Heels became one of the original teams to start the Southern Conference. They were a dominant force in and out of the league. The team finished with a winning record in each of the next 17 seasons. In its 32 years in the Southern Conference, North Carolina had only three losing seasons.

The 1923–24 season was a particularly special one. Led by senior forward/guard Cartwright Carmichael and sophomore forward Jack Cobb, North Carolina went undefeated with a 26–0 record. Years later, the Helms Foundation retroactively

CARMICHAEL AND COBB

Cartwright Carmichael and Jack Cobb were two of the most important players during North Carolina's first 25 years. The Tar Heels lost just 17 games over the five-season period in which the two played. Carmichael, who played from 1921 to 1924, became the first, first-team All-American athlete in University of North Carolina history in 1923. He was again named All-American the following year. Carmichael was such a good athlete that he also played baseball for the university.

Cobb played for the Tar Heels from 1923 to 1926. He was the first three-time All-America selection in University of North Carolina history. He was also named National Player of the Year in 1926. This honor led to him becoming the first Tar Heel to have his jersey retired by the school. Players did not wear numbers at the time. Through 2011, only eight players in the school's history have had their jersey or jersey number retired.

named that North Carolina team the national champion. The foundation was a group that decided who was the best college basketball team before the creation of the NCAA Tournament.

The Tar Heels built on-court rivalries with other local schools during their time in the Southern Conference. The Duke Blue Devils, the North Carolina State Wolfpack, and the Wake Forest Demon Deacons were also Southern Conference teams located in North Carolina. In 1953, those four North Carolina schools joined four other schools to start a new conference: the ACC. The other four teams were the Maryland Terrapins, the South Carolina Gamecocks, the Virginia Cavaliers, and the Clemson Tigers.

Frank McGuire had taken over as coach of the Tar Heels just one season before the move to the ACC. But he struggled in the new conference. North Carolina won its first ACC game 82–56 over South Carolina. But the Tar Heels

Lennie Rosenbluth (10) goes up for a layup in 1955. He holds the Tar Heels' season record for points with 895.

were just 21–21 during their first two ACC seasons. Things began to turn around after that. The Tar Heels went 18–5 during the 1955–56 season to earn a share of the ACC regular-season title. The NCAA Tournament was around at the time. However, only the winners from the conference tournaments participated.

The 1956–57 season would go down as one of the most memorable and important in team history. McGuire, in his fifth season as head coach, guided the team to an undefeated regular-season record of 24–0. Senior forward Lennie Rosenbluth led the team in scoring with 28 points per game. He was named National Player of the Year. North Carolina won the ACC regular-season and tournament titles to earn a spot in the 1957 NCAA Tournament.

The NCAA Tournament had only 23 teams at the time. North Carolina won its first three games to reach the Final Four in Kansas City, Missouri. The Tar Heels needed triple overtime to defeat the Michigan State Spartans 74–70 in the national semifinal. That set up a date with the Kansas Jayhawks and superstar center Wilt Chamberlain for the championship just one day later. Once again, North Carolina was forced to go to triple overtime. And once again, it prevailed. The Tar Heels escaped with a 54–53 victory.

"We were in great shape," North Carolina forward Pete Brennan said years later. "And we didn't believe in making excuses. . . . I guess we were too excited and too determined to think about fatigue."

"THE BLIND BOMBER"

George Glamack suffered from vision problems that made it difficult for him to focus on the hoop. But that did not stop the forward-center from becoming one of the most decorated Tar Heels basketball players ever. To make up for his impaired vision, "The Blind Bomber" used the painted lines on the court to aim for the rim. Glamack played for the Tar Heels from 1938 to 1941, and he was named National Player of the Year in both 1940 and 1941. In 1941, he averaged 20.6 points per game and led North Carolina to its first-ever appearance in the NCAA Tournament.

The Tar Heels had made it through another season without a loss, and they had their first official NCAA championship to show for it. The run to the championship became known as "McGuire's Miracle." But the trip to the Final Four in Kansas City was important for another reason, too. It was at that Final Four that McGuire met Dean Smith. At the time, Smith was an assistant coach for the Air Force Falcons. But soon he would become a household name in North Carolina and a national symbol of Tar Heel basketball.

North Carolina coach Dean Smith's 879 wins remained the third most in NCAA history through 2011.

3

DEAN'S DECADES

THE 1957 NATIONAL CHAMPIONSHIP WAS THE LAST TOURNAMENT SUCCESS THE TAR HEELS WOULD EXPERIENCE FOR A WHILE. THE BASKETBALL TEAM WAS ACCUSED OF VIOLATING NCAA RULES PRIOR TO THE 1960–61 SEASON. AS PUNISHMENT, THE TEAM WAS BANNED FROM PLAYING IN THE POSTSEASON THAT YEAR.

Later in the season, it was confirmed that some Tar Heels players had been bribed to shave points during games. That means the players accepted money from gamblers to not try as hard.

Following the 1960–61 season, coach Frank McGuire decided to accept an offer to coach in the NBA for the Philadelphia Warriors. But he left the program in capable hands. McGuire had hired Dean Smith as his assistant one year after meeting him at the 1957 Final Four. McGuire and North Carolina chancellor William Aycock both agreed that Smith was the right man to take over as head coach.

SMITH SIGNS SCOTT

Coach Dean Smith was well known for helping North Carolina on the court. But he also did a lot for the university's hometown, Chapel Hill, off of the court. One of Smith's most notable decisions was recruiting guard Charles Scott to attend North Carolina.

Scott became the first black athlete to receive a scholarship from North Carolina. When he first came to Chapel Hill in 1966, there was still some segregation in the southern parts of the United States. This meant that African-Americans were not given the same opportunities as others. But Smith refused to look at Scott's skin color as a factor.

"Coach Smith never really talked about integration," Scott said. "He always talked about me being part of the team." And Scott was an important part of the team from 1967 to 1970. He was a two-time All-American, and he averaged 22.1 points and 7.1 rebounds per game during his career.

The Tar Heels easily won Smith's first game, 80–46, against the Virginia Cavaliers. But success would not continue to come that easy. The team had only one winning season in Smith's first three years as coach.

Things finally started to turn for Smith and the Tar Heels. They started playing in a new building—Carmichael Auditorium—on December 4, 1965. They celebrated with an 82–68 victory over the William and Mary Indians. The wins started to pile up. And once again, the team found itself in the Associated Press rankings.

The Tar Heels returned to the top of the ACC in the 1966–67 season. That marked their first regular-season conference title under Smith. They then defeated their biggest rivals, the Duke Blue Devils, for Smith's first ACC Tournament championship. The team also qualified for the NCAA Tournament for the first time in eight seasons.

North Carolina defeated the Princeton Tigers and the Boston College Eagles to reach the Final Four. But the Tar Heels lost 76–62 to the Dayton Flyers in the national semifinals. The season ended with an 84–62 loss to the Houston Cougars in the third-place game.

The Tar Heels were back in the Final Four the next season. This time they beat the Ohio State Buckeyes in the national semifinals to return to the championship game. Their opponent was the University of California, Los Angeles Bruins. Superstar center Lew Alcindor led the Bruins. Later known as Kareem Abdul-Jabbar, Alcindor eventually became the NBA's all-time leading scorer. Alcindor proved to be too much for the Tar Heels to handle in 1968. He scored 34 points and had 16 rebounds in the final. Only two North Carolina players scored in double figures in the 78–55 loss.

Larry Miller, *left,* was the ACC Player of the Year for the Tar Heels in 1966–67 and 1967–68.

The Tar Heels found themselves back in the Final Four for the third straight season in 1968–69. But they once again came up short. The Purdue Boilermakers blew out the Tar Heels 92–65 in the national semifinals. And North Carolina was again soundly defeated in the third-place game 104–84 by the Drake Bulldogs.

The end of the 1960s had been eventful for the Tar Heels. They had made three straight trips to the Final Four. But they had come up short in the end each time. People started to wonder if Smith had what it took to win the big one.

The 1970s would offer no answers for those questioning Smith. Despite an entire decade of winning seasons, the Tar Heels could not capture a championship. In 1972, North Carolina lost to the Florida State Seminoles 79–75 in the national semifinals. Five years later, the Marquette Warriors defeated the Tar Heels 67–59 in the championship game.

The start of the 1980s looked to be the same. North Carolina once again made it to the championship game in 1981. And once again it lost. This time the Indiana Hoosiers beat the Tar Heels 63–50. Smith had taken the Tar Heels to the Final Four six times in his first 20 seasons as head coach. The result was three losses in the semifinals and three losses in the championship game.

Smith finally got his breakthrough in the 1981–82 season. Freshman guard Michael Jordan's famous jump shot with 15 seconds left helped North Carolina overcome superstar freshman center Patrick Ewing and the Georgetown Hoyas 63–62.

Talented players kept coming to play for Smith. Behind stars such as guard Kenny Smith, forward J. R. Reid, and center Brad Daugherty, the Tar Heels continued to make the NCAA Tournament year after year. But it

SMITH'S NEW SCHEME

One of the first things Dean Smith did as head coach was create an offense called the "Four Corners." The plan was to have his best dribbler—usually a guard—handle the ball at the free-throw line, and have the other four players in each corner of the offensive half of the court. Having the team so spread out made it difficult to stop. The Four Corners could be used to try and score points, or to let the clock tick down during tight games when North Carolina held a lead.

DEAN'S DECADES

would take them almost 10 years to again reach the Final Four. In 1991, they finally made it back. But Smith's second title would have to wait. The Tar Heels lost to the Kansas Jayhawks 79–73 in the semifinal.

The two teams again met in the Final Four just two years later. But this time it was the Tar Heels who would come out on top 76–68. Sophomore guard Donald Williams led the team with 25 points. And junior center Eric Montross scored 23. That set up the championship game against the Michigan Wolverines.

Michigan had lost to Duke in the national championship the previous year. A group of Wolverines nicknamed the "Fab Five" was hungry for redemption in 1993. Behind those five star sophomores—forwards Chris Webber, Juwan Howard, and Ray Jackson, and guards Jalen Rose and Jimmy King—Michigan had already defeated North Carolina in a tight game earlier that year.

The Final Four was played in the New Orleans Superdome. That was where the Tar Heels had won their title in 1982. North Carolina had a six-point lead at halftime. But the Tar Heels were up just 73–71 with 20 seconds

FABULOUS FORD

Phil Ford was one of the most popular and skilled Tar Heels to ever dribble a basketball. The guard, who played from 1974 to 1978, remained the second leading scorer in Tar Heels history in 2011, with 2,290 career points. Ford also was the first college player ever to score 2,000 points and have 600 assists in a career. The 1978 National Player of the Year thrived at running Dean Smith's famous "Four Corners" offense.

left. It was then that one of the most famous mistakes in college basketball history took place.

With less than 20 seconds to play, Webber grabbed the rebound off a North Carolina missed free throw. It appeared as if Webber traveled as he began taking the ball up court, but the referees did not call it. Webber made a bigger gaffe a few seconds later. He dribbled the ball into the North Carolina corner. With 11 seconds left he called a timeout. But Michigan had already used all of its timeouts. So a technical foul was called against Webber. Williams, who was North Carolina's leading scorer, hit both resulting free throws. The Tar Heels ended up winning the game 77–71. Smith and the Tar Heels were again on top.

DEAN'S DECADES

Jerry Stackhouse dunks the ball against the Kentucky Wildcats during the 1995 NCAA Tournament.

DEAN DEPARTS

DEAN SMITH WAS 62 YEARS OLD WHEN THE TAR HEELS DEFEATED THE MICHIGAN WOLVERINES FOR THE THIRD NCAA CHAMPIONSHIP IN SCHOOL HISTORY IN 1993. HE WAS GETTING OLDER, AND HIS COACHING TIME WAS RUNNING OUT. BUT HIS NORTH CAROLINA SQUADS STILL HAD A FEW MORE TOURNAMENT RUNS LEFT IN THEM.

Throughout the 1993–94 season, it looked like the Tar Heels were on their way to back-to-back national titles. Exciting freshmen such as guard Jerry Stackhouse and forward Rasheed Wallace joined the team. They helped lead North Carolina to a 24–6 regular-season record. Smith won his 800th game when the Tar Heels came from behind to beat the Wake Forest Demon Deacons in the ACC Tournament semifinals. North Carolina went on to win the final against the Virginia Cavaliers, 73–66. The Tar Heels then earned a number-one seed in the NCAA Tournament.

A LEGEND

Dean Smith is widely considered one of the best basketball coaches of all time. He ended his 36-year head coach career with a record of 879–254. That is the third most career wins for a coach as of the 2010–11 season. Smith had only one losing season during the entire time he coached in Chapel Hill. That was his first season, 1961–62. With Smith in charge, North Carolina finished as ACC regular-season champions 12 times and tied for first another five times. The Tar Heels also won the ACC Tournament 13 times during that span.

But perhaps the most impressive part of Smith's time at North Carolina was the team's 27 NCAA Tournament appearances. They were in the Final Four 11 times, and they won it all twice. In January 1986, North Carolina started playing in the Dean E. Smith Center, named after the legendary Tar Heels coach.

But their spectacular season soon came to a sudden halt. The Boston College Eagles upset the Tar Heels in the second round of the tournament. There would be no championship repeat in Chapel Hill.

Stackhouse and Wallace returned the next season. They were determined to get to the Final Four. And they did. But injuries got in the way of a championship. Wallace sprained his ankle during the ACC championship game. That was just five days before the start of the NCAA Tournament. He was able to return for the NCAA Tournament. But Stackhouse injured his leg in the first minute of the national semifinals against the Arkansas Razorbacks. North Carolina was unable to overcome the injuries to two of its top scorers. The season ended with a 75–68 loss to Arkansas.

Smith and the Tar Heels would have another memorable run just two years later. But the beginning of the 1996–97

North Carolina's Vince Carter goes up for a basket against North Carolina State during the 1998 ACC Tournament.

season did not go well for North Carolina. The team lost its first game of the season 83–72 to the Arizona Wildcats. It then lost its first three ACC games. But behind stars such as sophomore forwards Antawn Jamison and Vince Carter, and junior guard Shammond Williams, the team was still able to finish the regular season with a 21–6 record. The Tar Heels won the ACC Tournament and headed into the NCAA Tournament as a number-one seed.

North Carolina beat the Colorado Buffaloes 73–56 in the second round of the NCAA Tournament. It was Smith's 877th career win. That broke the record previously held by former Kentucky Wildcats coach Adolph Rupp.

DEAN DEPARTS

Smith was known for shying away from attention. He always wanted the spotlight to be on his players instead of on himself. The moments after his record-breaking victory were no different.

"I've been fortunate to have had some great players, some good players who became better, and some that helped the team and didn't play a lot," Smith said. "They all share in this moment."

The Tar Heels then beat California and Louisville to reach the Final Four. There they faced Arizona for the second time that season. And just like in the first game, the Wildcats were too good for the Tar Heels. North Carolina lost 66–58. It would be Smith's last game as coach.

Age was catching up to Smith. On October 9, 1997, he announced his retirement at age 66. "If I can't give this team that enthusiasm, I said I would get out," he said. "And that's honestly how I feel. I'm the luckiest guy in the world, and I've said that, to be in Chapel Hill, to be at the University of North Carolina, with this faculty, this student body."

ANTAWN JAMISON

Antawn Jamison was one of the most important players during North Carolina's back-to-back appearances in the Final Four in 1997 and 1998. During a time when the program was going through changes at the coaching position, Jamison was a stable force on the court. He won the Naismith Award, which is given to the national player of the year, after the 1997–98 season. That season he averaged 22.2 points and 10.5 rebounds per game. It was the first time a North Carolina player had averaged a double-double since Mitch Kupchak did it in 1975–76.

Forward Antawn Jamison goes up against the Duke Blue Devils during the 1998 ACC championship game.

Bill Guthridge replaced Smith as coach before the start of the 1997–98 season. Guthridge was no stranger to the North Carolina program. He had been one of Smith's assistants for 30 years before becoming head coach. He only coached North Carolina for three seasons, but he still left an impact on the team.

The team still had several of the talented players from the squad that had lost to Arizona in the Final Four, including Jamison, Williams, and Carter. The Tar Heels went 34–4 and made the Final Four for the second straight season. But also for the second straight season, they lost one game before the championship. They went down 65–59 to the Utah Utes.

It was a promising start for Guthridge. He was named National Coach of the Year for taking the team to the Final Four in his first season. After another promising season in 1998–99, the Tar Heels were upset in the first round of the tournament by the Weber State Wildcats. But Guthridge had the team back in the Final Four the next year.

Unfortunately for North Carolina, the results were the same. The Tar Heels went down to the Florida Gators 71–59. Freshman guard Joseph Forte and junior center Brendan Haywood were the only two Tar Heels to score in double figures in the game.

Although Guthridge had taken the Tar Heels to two Final Fours in his first three years as head coach, he decided to retire in June 2000.

KNIGHT'S ACCOLADES

"His being able to do that and do it at a single institution, do it through all the years without ever having a problem with any kind of recruiting violation or probation, is a very singular accomplishment in college basketball. I think it's a great achievement, indicative of a guy who really knows how to coach and has decided from day one that things are going to be done the absolute right way." —Bob Knight, record-holder for most wins by a men's NCAA Division I coach, speaking about Dean Smith

Former Tar Heel player Matt Doherty was chosen as his replacement. "When you're handed a program that's been to six of the last 10 Final Fours, you can see it as pressure or as an opportunity," Doherty said. "I think it's pretty cool."

Doherty had his sights set on continuing the tradition of success at North Carolina. But he was in for a bumpy ride.

DEAN DEPARTS

Through 2011, Roy Williams has won two national championships with the Tar Heels.

ROY TO THE RESCUE

WITH A NEW CENTURY CAME A NEW COACH AT NORTH CAROLINA. MATT DOHERTY TOOK OVER BEFORE THE START OF THE 2000–01 SEASON. MOST OF THE FINAL FOUR TEAM FROM THE PREVIOUS SEASON WAS BACK. AND IT WAS BUSINESS AS USUAL FOR THE TAR HEELS.

North Carolina finished 26–7 and won the ACC regular season title. Sophomore guard Joseph Forte and junior center Brendan Haywood again led the team in scoring. They also led the team to the NCAA Tournament. But the Penn State Nittany Lions upset the Tar Heels in the second round. It was a sign of bad things to come.

North Carolina hit rock bottom during the next season. It was the worst basketball season in school history. The team finished just 8–20. After losing their first three games of the season, the Tar Heels went just 4–12 in ACC play and finished tied for last in the conference. They missed the NCAA

Tournament for the first time since 1974. Perhaps the most embarrassing points of the season were North Carolina's performances against archrival Duke. The Tar Heels lost the two games against their biggest rival by a combined 54 points. They allowed opponents to score 78.9 points per game during the season. That ranked them 300th out of 321 schools.

The next season was a little better for Doherty. But it would still be his last. The team went 19–16. North Carolina once again finished seventh in the ACC and did not make the NCAA Tournament. But the team was young. Guards Rashad McCants and Raymond Felton, and forward Sean May were all freshmen. Along with sophomore forward Jawad Williams, they were the team's four leading scorers. Even though Doherty had overseen two of the worst years in team history, he left the program with some talented players.

North Carolina turned to another former assistant coach to lead them. After serving as an assistant at North Carolina from 1978 to 1988, Roy Williams had gone 418–101 during 15 seasons as head coach of the Kansas Jayhawks. In 2003, he came back to his home state of North Carolina to coach the Tar Heels. It would turn out to be a good decision.

With a new coach and a group of talented young players with a season of experience, North Carolina was able to get back to the NCAA Tournament in Williams's first year. The Tar Heels were knocked out in a close, second-round game by the talented Texas Longhorns. But the pieces were starting to fall back into place for North Carolina.

Expectations were high heading into the 2004–05 season. North Carolina started the season with a loss—a shocking upset to the Santa Clara

The Tar Heels' Raymond Felton drives past Illinois' Dee Brown during the 2005 NCAA Tournament finals.

Broncos. But the Tar Heels rattled off 14 straight wins after that. They finished first in the ACC during the regular season. They then headed into the NCAA Tournament with a number-one seed.

North Carolina opened the tournament with easy wins against the Oakland Golden Grizzlies and the Iowa State Cyclones. The team then had

to win two tight games against the Villanova Wildcats and the Wisconsin Badgers. That put the Tar Heels back in the Final Four.

North Carolina played the Michigan State Spartans in the semifinals. The Tar Heels found themselves down five points at halftime. But they outscored Michigan State by 21 in the second half. Behind 22 points from May—18 of which came in the second half—and 20 from Jawad Williams, North Carolina advanced to the final with an 87–71 victory.

The only team left between them and a championship was the Illinois Fighting Illini. Illinois had lost only once all season and had been ranked at the top of the Associated Press poll for months. Still, North Carolina stormed out to a 13-point lead at halftime. But Illinois fought back to tie the game at 70 with 2:39 to go. North Carolina would not let them get another score.

The Tar Heels won 75–70. Roy Williams had won a title in just his second year as North Carolina's head coach.

May capped off an incredible tournament by leading the team with 26 points and 10 rebounds in that championship game. He made 10 of 11 shots. And he was named the tournament's Most Outstanding Player.

North Carolina lost its top five scorers and rebounders after the 2005 title to graduation and the NBA Draft. But a new crop of freshmen started a new generation of winning. Forward Tyler Hansbrough led the team with 18.9 points and 7.8 rebounds per game. And even though the Tar Heels lost in the second round of the NCAA Tournament to the George Mason Patriots, the pieces were in place for another championship run.

Freshman forward Brandan Wright and guards Wayne Ellington and Ty Lawson joined Hansbrough the next year. The three new players were the second, third, and fourth leading scorers after Hansbrough during the 2006–07 season. The Tar Heels finished first in the ACC and won the conference tournament. They made it to the Elite Eight before losing 96–84 in overtime to the Georgetown Hoyas.

The Tar Heels entered the next season poised to take it a step further. Their younger players had grown with experience. Hansbrough averaged career highs with 22.6 points and 10.2 rebounds per game. He was named National Player of the Year. The Tar Heels again breezed through the regular season and the ACC Tournament. They only lost twice heading into the NCAA Tournament. This time, the Tar Heels made the Final Four. But there they were blown out by Williams's old team, the Kansas Jayhawks, 84–66.

"PSYCHO T"

Tyler Hansbrough was known for his hustle and determination on the court. His aggression and the fact that he never seemed to get tired earned him the nickname "Psycho T." Those attributes also helped him become one of the best players in ACC history.

The Poplar Bluff, Missouri, native made an immediate impact when he started playing at North Carolina during the 2005–06 season. On February 15, 2006, he scored an ACC freshman record 40 points against the Georgia Tech Yellow Jackets. He would go on to score more than anybody in North Carolina history. On December 18, 2008, Hansbrough passed Phil Ford as North Carolina's all-time leading scorer. Later that season he would become the ACC's all-time leading scorer. Hansbrough left North Carolina with 2,872 points, and he is one of the eight players to have his number retired at Chapel Hill.

Despite the chance to be chosen in the NBA Draft, Hansbrough came back for his senior year. He wanted to win a title. North Carolina was again a number-one seed in the NCAA Tournament. And this time, it would not be denied. An 89–72 win over Michigan State brought the players their first championship. It was the second for Williams as coach. The Tar Heels were unstoppable during one of the most dominant NCAA Tournament runs of all time. They won each of their six tournament games by at least 12 points.

The happiness of winning was soon be erased by the disappointment of defeat. With Hansbrough, Lawson, Ellington, and Wright all gone, the Tar Heels had a rough 2009–10 season. They went 20–17 and finished 10th in the ACC. They missed the NCAA Tournament for the first time under Williams.

But champions do not stay down for long. Williams made a big change in the

middle of the 2010–11 season. He put freshman guard Kendall Marshall in the starting lineup. With Marshall running the show, the team lost just three more games before the NCAA Tournament. Once there, North Carolina made it to the Elite Eight before losing to the Kentucky Wildcats.

Still, the future looks bright in Chapel Hill. Dean Smith's 36 seasons established the Tar Heels as one of the most exciting and skilled teams in the nation. And Williams has already proved capable of carrying on those traditions.

TIMELINE

On January 27, the North Carolina Tar Heels defeat Virginia Christian 42–21 in their first ever game.

On March 4, the Tar Heels complete their first undefeated season by beating the Alabama Crimson Tide 26–18 to go to 26–0.

North Carolina makes its first appearance in the NCAA Tournament.

On March 21, a 57–49 victory over New York University gives North Carolina its first NCAA Tournament win. The Tar Heels would also advance to their first Final Four that year.

On December 1, the Tar Heels win 70–50 over the Citadel Bulldogs in Frank McGuire's first game as head coach.

1911 1924 1941 1946 1952

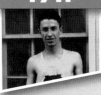

On March 29, freshman guard Michael Jordan hits a game-winning jump shot with 15 seconds left to secure a 63–62 NCAA final victory over the Georgetown Hoyas. It is Smith's first championship in four appearances.

On March 30, the Tar Heels lose 63–50 to the Indiana Hoosiers in the NCAA final.

On January 18, the Tar Heels beat the rival Duke Blue Devils 95–92 in the first game played in the Dean E. Smith Center.

On April 5, North Carolina defeats the Michigan Wolverines 77–71 for the NCAA championship. It is Smith's second title.

On October 9, Smith retires as the all-time wins leader in NCAA history. Assistant Bill Guthridge is hired as a replacement and wins National Coach of the Year.

1981 1982 1986 1993 1997

North Carolina leaves the Southern Conference to become one of the founding members of the ACC.

On March 23, the Tar Heels defeat the Kansas Jayhawks 54–53 in triple overtime to complete an undefeated season and win North Carolina's first NCAA championship.

On December 2, North Carolina beats the Virginia Cavaliers 80–46 in Dean Smith's first game as head coach.

On March 23, North Carolina loses to the UCLA Bruins 78–55 in the NCAA championship.

On March 28, North Carolina loses 67–59 to the Marquette Warriors in the NCAA final.

1953   1957   1961   1968   1977

North Carolina has its worst season ever. The team finishes with a record of 8–20 and misses the NCAA Tournament for the first time since 1974.

On April 14, former North Carolina assistant Roy Williams takes over as head coach two weeks after Matt Doherty resigns.

On April 4, the Tar Heels beat the Illinois Fighting Illini 75–70 for the school's fourth NCAA championship. It is Williams's first title as a head coach.

On April 6, North Carolina defeats the Michigan State Spartans 89–72 for the program's fifth title, its second in five years.

On November 28, North Carolina beats the College of Charleston Cougars 74–69 to give Williams his 200th win as head coach of the Tar Heels.

2002   2003   2005   2009   2010

QUICK STATS

PROGRAM INFO
University of North Carolina
Tar Heels (1911–)

NCAA TOURNAMENT FINALS
(WINS IN BOLD)
1946, **1957**, 1968, 1977, 1981, **1982,
1993**, **2005**, **2009**

OTHER ACHIEVEMENTS
Final Fours: 18
NCAA Tournaments: 42
ACC Tournament Titles: 17

KEY PLAYERS
(POSITION(S); YEARS WITH TEAM)
Cartwright Carmichael (G/F;
    1921–24)
Vince Carter (G/F; 1995–98)
Jack Cobb (F; 1923–26)
Billy Cunningham (F; 1962–65)
Raymond Felton (G; 2002–05)
Phil Ford (G; 1974–78)
George Glamack (F/C; 1938–41)
Tyler Hansbrough (F; 2005–09)

Antawn Jamison (F; 1995–98)
Michael Jordan (G/F; 1981–84)
Sean May (C; 2002–05)
Bob McAdoo (C/F; 1971–72)
Lennie Rosenbluth (F; 1954–57)
James Worthy (F; 1979–82)

KEY COACHES
Frank McGuire (1952–61):
    164–58; 5–1 (NCAA Tournament)
Dean Smith (1961–97):
    879–254; 65–27 (NCAA Tournament)
Roy Williams (2003–):
    225–62; 24–5 (NCAA Tournament)

HOME ARENA
Dean E. Smith Center (1986–)

* All statistics through 2010–11 season

The nickname "Tar Heel" has a curious history. In the 1700s, England used to make and send home tar from the large pine tree forests of North Carolina. The process was messy. People would end up stepping in the tar and tracking it around on the bottoms of their shoes. But it is believed that the specific term "Tar Heel" was first used during the Civil War in 1863 to describe brave troops from North Carolina. What used to be a negative way to describe people from the state had become a source of pride.

Billy Cunningham, whose jumping ability earned him the nickname "The Kangaroo Kid," holds the NCAA record for the most consecutive games with a double-double. He had a double-double in 40 straight games between 1962–64.

"We share the same dry cleaners. . . . There is no other area like this. It produces things, situations, feelings that you can't talk to other people about. Because they have no understanding of it." —Duke head coach Mike Krzyzewski on Duke's rivalry with North Carolina. The schools are just miles apart.

"He is the greatest coach. If he retired tomorrow, I would vote for him for the Hall of Fame. He told us he would bring us a championship, and we did it as a team." —North Carolina guard Raymond Felton speaking about Roy Williams after winning 2005 title

GLOSSARY

assist

A pass that leads directly to a made basket.

attendance

The number of fans at a particular game or who come to watch a team play during a particular season.

conference

In basketball, a group of teams that plays against each other each season.

draft

A system used by professional sports leagues to select new players in order to spread incoming talent among all teams. The NBA Draft is held each June.

double-double

When a player achieves double digits in two categories, such as points, assists, rebounds, blocks, or steals, in one game.

overtime

An extra period in a basketball game that is played to determine a winner when regulation play ends in a tie.

rebound

To secure the basketball after a missed shot.

recruiting

The process of convincing a star athlete to join one's team.

retire

To officially end one's career. If a team retires a jersey number, no future player is allowed to wear it for that team.

rival

An opponent that brings out great emotion in a team, its fans, and its players.

scholarship

Financial assistance awarded to students to help them pay for school. Top athletes earn scholarships to represent a college through its sports teams.

seed

In basketball, a ranking system used for tournaments. The best teams earn a number-one seed.

FOR MORE INFORMATION

FURTHER READING

Brewer, Rick. *University of North Carolina Basketball Vault*. Atlanta, GA: Whitman Publishing, 2008.

Fowler, Scott. *What It Means to Be a Tar Heel: Roy Williams and North Carolina's Greatest Players*. Chicago, IL: Triumph Books, 2010.

Williams, Roy and Tim Crothers. *Hard Work: A Life On and Off the Court*. Chapel Hill, NC: Algonquin Books, 2009.

WEB LINKS

To learn more about the North Carolina Tar Heels, visit ABDO Publishing Company online at **www.abdopublishing.com**. Web sites about the Tar Heels are featured on our Book Links page. These links are routinely monitored and updated to provide the most current information available.

PLACES TO VISIT

The Carolina Basketball Museum
450 Skipper Bowles Drive
Chapel Hill, NC 27514
919-843-9921
http://tarheelblue.cstv.com/museum/index.html

This interactive museum includes videos and memorabilia from throughout the history of the North Carolina basketball program. Learn about past and present coaches and players, and relive some of the best games in which the Tar Heels ever played.

Dean E. Smith Center
300 Skipper Bowles Drive
Chapel Hill, NC 27514
919-962-7777
http://tarheelblue.cstv.com/facilities/unc-smith-center.html

This has been North Carolina's home arena since 1986. Named after the legendary Tar Heels' coach, it is often called "the Dean Dome." There are no tours, but the public is allowed to visit the second and third floors Monday through Friday during the day.

INDEX

ABOUT THE AUTHOR

Alex Monnig is a freelance journalist from St. Louis, Missouri. He graduated with his master's degree from the University of Missouri in May 2010. During his career he has spent time covering sporting events around the world, including the 2008 Olympic Games in China, the 2010 Commonwealth Games in India, and the 2010 Rugby World Cup in New Zealand.